ESSENTIAL **DK** COMPUTERS

ENTERTAINMENT

HAVING FUN
ON YOUR PC

ABOUT THIS BOOK

Having Fun On Your PC is an easy-to-use guide
that provides an introduction to the different ways in which
you can use your computer for entertainment and leisure.

WHILE YOUR COMPUTER IS
undoubtedly a powerful
business and educational tool,
it also offers you the chance to interact in
a whole host of exciting and inspirational
fun experiences. This book provides an
antidote to the everyday tasks your
computer undertakes, and explains in
simple terms how to get involved with
multimedia.

Whether you want to play games, use
CD-ROMs, watch movies, or create your
own computer-generated pictures, *Having
Fun On Your PC* provides simple
instructions to help get you started.

Each chapter of the book is intended
to stand alone, so you can choose either to
work through the book systematically, or
to turn straight to the sections that
interest you.

The chapters and the subsections present
the information using step-by-step

sequences. Virtually every step is
accompanied by an illustration showing
how your screen should look at each stage.

The book contains several features to
help you understand both what is
happening and what you need to do.

Command keys, such as ENTER and
CTRL, are shown in these rectangles:
Enter↵ and Ctrl, so that there's no
confusion, for example, over whether
you should press that key or type the
letters "ctrl."

Cross-references are shown in the text as
left- or right-hand page icons: ⌐ and ⌐.
The page number and the reference are
shown at the foot of the page.

In addition to the step-by-step sections,
there are boxes that explain a feature in
detail, and tip boxes that provide
alternative methods. Finally, at the back,
you will find a glossary of common terms,
and a comprehensive index.

ESSENTIAL DK COMPUTERS

ENTERTAINMENT

HAVING FUN ON YOUR PC

ANDY ASHDOWN

A Dorling Kindersley Book

Dorling Kindersley
LONDON, NEW YORK, SYDNEY, DELHI,
PARIS, MUNICH, and JOHANNESBURG

Produced for Dorling Kindersley Limited by
Design Revolution, Queens Park Villa,
30 West Drive, Brighton, East Sussex BN2 2GE

EDITORIAL DIRECTOR Ian Whitelaw
SENIOR DESIGNER Andy Ashdown
PROJECT EDITOR Julie Whitaker

MANAGING EDITOR Adele Hayward
SENIOR MANAGING ART EDITOR Nigel Duffield
PROJECT EDITOR Mark Wallace
DTP DESIGNER Julian Dams
PRODUCTION CONTROLLER Michelle Thomas

Published in Great Britain in 2001 by
Dorling Kindersley Limited,
9 Henrietta Street, London WC2E 8PS

2 4 6 8 10 9 7 5 3 1

A CIP catalog record for this book is available from the British Library.

ISBN 0-7513-1305-X

Color reproduced by Colourscan, Singapore
Printed in Italy by Graphicom

For our complete
catalog visit
www.dk.com

CONTENTS

INTRODUCTION

Your PC may be highly efficient at word processing and spreadsheets, but these are just its "daytime" duties. Its true power, and attraction, lies in multimedia and entertainment.

BRINGING YOUR PC TO LIFE

Games, CD-ROMs, DVDs, and the internet all play a large part in having fun on your computer. All of these, plus others such as movie-making and animation, fall under the broader category of "multimedia."

MULTIMEDIA BONANZA
Without a doubt, the PC's multimedia capabilities have been instrumental in the sheer volume of recent PC sales, and the dramatic fall in some hardware prices. In fact, the majority of today's personal computers are purchased solely for game-playing and other leisure pursuits. The result of this has been the creation of a great wealth of recreational activities, all waiting to be discovered by the imaginative PC user.

INTERACTIVE CD-ROMS
For education, practical pursuits, or just plain and simple fun, CD-ROMs provide an exciting and interactive spin on everyday subjects ⌐|. Companies often use CD-ROMs to advertise their services, and you can sometimes obtain free software and other benefits.

WHAT PART DOES THE INTERNET PLAY?

While it is not essential to have an internet connection to use your PC for leisure (you can still play games, watch DVD movies, and use drawing programs), there is certainly no doubt that it is an advantage, and opens up a host of opportunities. The internet not only provides its own unique forms of entertainment, such as online gaming and new movie trailers, but can also act as a valuable resource of information and software.

MUSIC

Your PC can become a powerful music tool, whether you are simply listening to CDs ⬐, or downloading songs from the internet.

FILM AND VIDEO

With the right hardware you can use your computer to watch the latest DVD releases ⬐. You can even connect to the internet sites of major Hollywood film studios and watch blockbuster movie trailers online ⬐.

CREATIVITY

Put your home PC to creative use in any area of art and design ⬐, or personalize your computer completely with customized icons and sounds ⬐.

GAMES

From simple card games ⬐ to the most complex multiplayer action adventures ⬐, a computer can open up whole new worlds to be explored. And far from being an antisocial activity, you can play against other people worldwide by connecting to gaming websites.

GAMES CONSOLES

Although not strictly regarded as computers, games consoles are certainly heading in the same direction. The most recent models boast internal modems so that you can play online against other competitors. This has meant that the consoles themselves can also be used with the internet and to send emails – and you need nothing more than a standard television set and a phone line.

SEGA DREAMCAST

The Sega Dreamcast includes an internal 56K modem that allows you to play your favorite games online with other Dreamcast users.

*• Handheld
controller*

Look out for...
The Microsoft X-Box, a radical new games console that promises to have even more exciting features than the Sega Dreamcast and Playstation 2.

SONY PLAYSTATION 2

The Playstation 2 is equipped to offer a truly rounded home entertainment experience. In addition to playing games, you can also use the console to listen to music CDs and watch films on DVD.

KEEPING UP-TO-DATE

The computer entertainment industry – games manufacturers especially – are under constant pressure to launch the biggest, fastest, and best software and games as soon as possible, and before anyone else. This is good news for the consumer, as you can expect a constant onslaught of top quality entertainment, all accessible through your PC. The flexible, upgradeable nature of your computer means that you can experience up-to-the-minute news and previews through CD-ROMs and the internet, and modify your PC to cope as technology evolves.

SOME POPULAR GAMING WEBSITES

www.gamecenter.com
www.gamesdomain.com
www.gameproworld.com
http://games.yahoo.com
www.happypuppy.com
www.microsoft.com/games
www.pcgamers.net
www.zdnet.com/gamespot
www.zone.com

www.gamecenter.com
Most gaming sites offer reviews, tips, cheats, and free downloads.

Reprinted with permission from CNET, Inc., © 1995-2000

SUBSCRIBING TO MAGAZINES

The internet is a good source of current news, views, and previews. However, there are also a great many computer and gaming magazines available each month – most of which carry a CD-ROM or DVD disk on the cover. These disks usually provide trial versions of software and games, giving you the opportunity to try out the latest releases before you buy them.

HARDWARE

You will find that there are many additional accessories that you can purchase for your PC. None of them is essential, but they can enhance your entertainment and gaming experiences.

PREPARING YOUR PC FOR ENTERTAINMENT

To really enjoy a movie or music CD at home, you would think about getting the biggest TV screen possible, along with the best music system and the loudest surround-sound speakers available. The same rules apply to your PC, and, although a lack of the items mentioned in this chapter would not prevent you from using your PC for entertainment, their addition will certainly enhance your experience.

THE MULTIMEDIA PC

Most manufacturers are aware that their PCs will be used for multimedia. As a result, most supply at least a set of stereo speakers with their computers. You will also find that the inclusion of an internal modem and a sizeable color monitor is now usually standard, and these are all highly desirable components for a good entertainment setup. However, there are further items that you can add, such as gaming controllers and additional speakers.

Computer •
Ideally your PC should have a CD-ROM or DVD-ROM drive and an internal modem.

Color monitor
As incredible as it may seem, computer monitors are available with screens as large as 37 inches (94 cms) – but at a price.

Steering wheel controller •
This accessory provides more natural control of driving simulations.

12 **Adding Controllers to Your PC**

DO I NEED TO UPGRADE MY COMPUTER?

Most modern computers are sold with multimedia as a key integral feature, and they are often bundled with free games and CD-ROMs. Therefore, if you have recently bought a home PC, it should have been supplied with enough processing power and hard drive space to cope with such demanding things as games and video. If you are venturing into the world of computer entertainment with a slightly older machine, it is worth checking the system specification to make sure you have the necessary power available. The minimum requirements listed here will enable you to operate all the features mentioned in this book, but the more power you have, the better the performance – especially with multimedia.

- 300MHz processor
- 64Mb of RAM
- 3Gb of hard drive space
- 32-bit graphics card
- Color monitor
- 56K modem

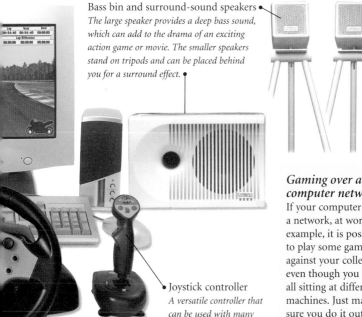

Bass bin and surround-sound speakers
The large speaker provides a deep bass sound, which can add to the drama of an exciting action game or movie. The smaller speakers stand on tripods and can be placed behind you for a surround effect.

Joystick controller
A versatile controller that can be used with many games and is especially suited to flying simulations.

Gaming over a computer network
If your computer is on a network, at work for example, it is possible to play some games against your colleagues, even though you are all sitting at different machines. Just make sure you do it outside office hours!

ADDING CONTROLLERS TO YOUR PC

To really enhance your multimedia experience – especially if you become seriously interested in computer gaming – you can invest in some of the many control accessories that are available. These additions include things such as joysticks and steering wheels, all of which provide an added realism and enhanced level of control to the games you are playing. Simply plug the controller of your choice into a port on your computer, perform a simple configuration process 🗋, and you are ready to fly a fighter plane or drive a Formula 1 racing car!

STEERING WHEELS

Obviously intended for use with driving simulations, some steering wheels also come with a set of foot pedals for the accelerator and the brake, giving you a very realistic driving experience. Other controls, such as the gearshift, are positioned on the steering column and on the wheel itself.

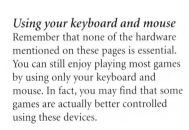

Using your keyboard and mouse
Remember that none of the hardware mentioned on these pages is essential. You can still enjoy playing most games by using only your keyboard and mouse. In fact, you may find that some games are actually better controlled using these devices.

Testing and configuring your controllers

GAMEPADS

If you are familiar with using a games console ⌐, then you may want to add this style of controller to your PC. The units are handheld, and have a variety of thumb-operated buttons that can be configured to perform particular actions.

JOYSTICKS

Joysticks have been around almost as long as computer games themselves. They still remain incredibly versatile controllers. Not only do they provide sensitive control for flight simulators; you can also use them for most other games.

TESTING AND CONFIGURING YOUR CONTROLLERS

Windows 98 provides a control panel for testing and configuring any controller that you connect to your PC. With the controller connected, click on the **Start** menu and select **Control Panel** from the **Settings** menu. Double-click on the **Game Controllers** icon and, when the window opens, highlight your controller in the list under the **General** tab. Click on **Properties** and use the options given under the **Settings** and **Test** tabs to ensure your controller is working correctly.

⌐8 **Games Consoles**

FUN WITH WINDOWS 98

To begin having fun on your PC, you need nothing more than
your Windows 98 operating system. Windows 98 will give you
an idea of the joys that are waiting to be discovered.

DISCOVERING MULTIMEDIA

Windows 98 offers some multimedia
facilities to get you started, including a
music CD player ⬚ and Windows Media
Player ⬚, a program that allows you to
watch video and live broadcasts over the
internet. You will also find that there are
some simple games available ⬚. However,

none of these really gives an accurate
picture of the true possibilities of your
computer. A good way of discovering what
is available is to take a look at the
Windows 98 CD, which includes some
interactive previews and demonstrations of
Microsoft software and games.

1 LAUNCHING THE INTERACTIVE CD

● Click on the **Start** button
and select **Programs** from
the pop-up menu, followed
by **Accessories**, then
Entertainment.
● Within the **Enter-
tainment** menu, select
Interactive CD Sampler.

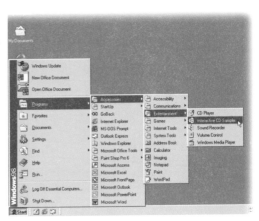

Entertainment menu
This also gives you
access to the **Volume
Control** and the **Sound
Recorder** ⬚.

 Playing a Music CD 17

 Using Windows Media Player 18

Playing Windows 98 Games 21

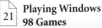 **Recording Sounds** 64

2 INSERTING THE WINDOWS 98 CD

● When prompted, insert the Windows 98 CD into your computer, and click the **OK** button.

3 STARTING THE CD-ROM

● The Windows 98 CD-ROM will open.
● Click on the icon for the **Interactive CD Sampler.**

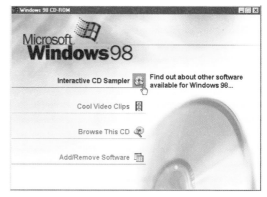

4 FIRST TIME USE OF THE CD-ROM

● If you haven't used the CD Sampler before, you will have to accept a license agreement and install some software on to your computer.
● Click on the **Next** button and follow the simple instructions onscreen to install the Microsoft Interactive CD Sampler onto your computer.

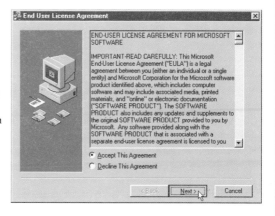

5 VIEWING THE CD SAMPLER

● Once the installation is complete, the CD Sampler will launch.

● Click on a category, for example **Games.**

● You can return to this screen later to view the other categories.

6 PREVIEWING A GAME

● In the **Games** section, there are a number of previews and trial versions for you to install and play.

● Hold your cursor over one of the graphics to hear a voice-over explaining the game, then click to open the options.

● You can either watch a preview or play part of the game.

EXITING THE CD SAMPLER

To close the CD Sampler, click on **Exit** in the top right of the screen and confirm that you really want to exit the CD. You will be returned to the main Windows 98 CD-ROM menu screen, which you can exit by clicking on the **Close (X)** button in the top right-hand corner.

PLAYING A MUSIC CD

One of the easiest ways of exploiting the entertainment potential of your computer is to use the CD-ROM drive to play conventional music CDs. Why not mix business with pleasure and have some of your favorite music playing in the background while you work? If you have added some multimedia speakers to your PC setup ⌐, then you might be pleasantly surprised by the sound quality. In addition to simply playing CDs, the CD Player software provided with Windows 98 also offers some very useful features that help you to create your own playlists and manage your music collection – experiment with the options in the menus.

1 LAUNCHING CD PLAYER

● Click on the **Start** button and select **Programs** from the pop-up menu, followed by **Accessories**, then **Entertainment.**
● Within the **Entertainment** menu, select **CD Player.**

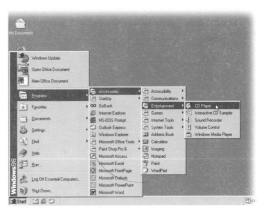

2 PLAYING THE MUSIC CD

● After the CD Player has launched, insert your music CD into your computer's CD-ROM drive.
● Click on the **Play** button.

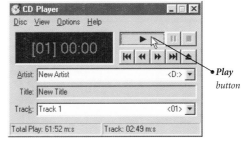

● *Play button*

3 PLAYING A DIFFERENT TRACK

● Just like a conventional CD player, you can use the **Skip**, **Pause**, and **Stop** buttons, or go straight to your favorite songs by highlighting them in the **Track** list.

USING WINDOWS MEDIA PLAYER

Windows Media Player is a multimedia player that allows you to watch and listen to video and audio files. The most exciting aspect of this is online viewing, which allows you to watch broadcasts – sometimes live – "streamed" over the internet to your computer. You can keep up-to-date with the latest news or view anything from a live music concert to a solar eclipse by selecting the relevant link in a website.

1 LAUNCHING MEDIA PLAYER

● Click on the **Start** button and select **Programs** from the pop-up menu, followed by **Accessories**, **Entertainment**, then **Windows Media Player**.

● **Windows Media Player** will open.

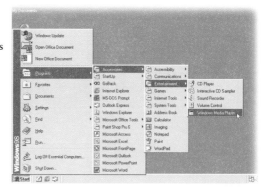

2 SELECTING A FAVORITE SITE

● One of the easiest ways to become familiar with the Media Player format is to select one of the existing links to internet sites.

● Click on the **Favorites** menu and highlight one of the media companies in the list.

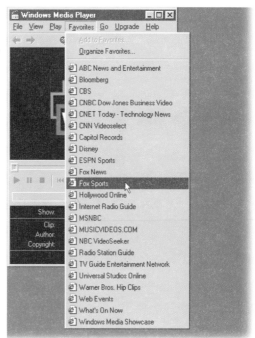

3 SETTING YOUR PLAYER OPTIONS

● Your internet browser will open automatically, taking you directly to a web page that offers video clips.

● Before viewing anything, you need to confirm what media player you are using and your modem speed.

● Click on the link labeled **Player Options** or **Video Options** (some sites may take you to the relevant page automatically).

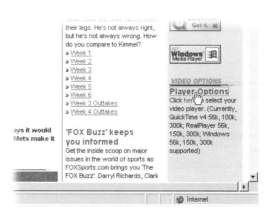

● A window will open offering you a range of choices.

● Click in the radio buttons to confirm that you are using Windows Media Player at your particular modem speed (this is usually 56K but could be higher depending on your computer setup).

● Click on the **Set Video Player** button to implement the settings.

● Close the window, if it does not close automatically, by clicking on the X button in the top right corner.

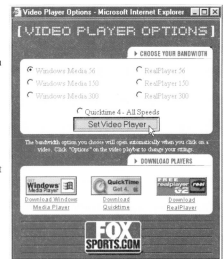

4 SELECTING A VIDEO

● When you return to the web page offering video footage, click on a link, a picture, or a **Play** button (these will differ depending on the site you chose).

5 WATCHING THE VIDEO

● The site will utilize the Windows Media Player facility of your computer to play the video. This will either appear in a pop-up window, or within the browser itself.

•You can play, pause, stop, rewind, or fast forward the video using these controls

PLAYING WINDOWS 98 GAMES

Windows 98 offers four standard games with the operating system, three of which are card games. Although very basic, these games provide a good grounding in computer gaming, and their simplicity can sometimes prove strangely addictive!

LAUNCHING A GAME

● Click on the **Start** button and select **Programs** from the pop-up menu, followed by **Accessories**, and then **Games**.
● Within the **Games** menu, select either **FreeCell**, **Hearts**, **Solitaire**, or **Minesweeper**.
● The game will launch.
● Now turn to the following pages to find out how to play each of the games.

FREECELL

● When **Freecell** opens, select **New Game** from the **Game** menu.
● A randomly chosen game, indicated by a number in the title bar, will appear on screen.

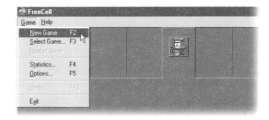

Finding out more…
You can view more of the rules, as well as strategies and tips for these games, by selecting **Help Topics** from the **Help** menu.

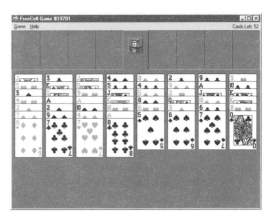

HOW TO PLAY FREECELL

This is a single-player game, the object being to transfer all the cards from the playing area at the bottom of the screen to the four home cells situated in the top right of the screen. A home cell must contain all the cards from one suit only, stacked in ascending order. The four cells in the top left of the screen are free cells, to be used as placeholders. Click on a card at the bottom of one of the dealt columns, then click on the cell you want to move it to. Aces, being the lowest ranked card, can move straight to a home cell from the bottom of a column. Thereafter, cards can be moved to the home cells either in ascending order from the bottom of the columns, or from a free cell, if you have placed a card there temporarily (a free cell can only be occupied by one card at a time). You can also move a card from a free cell, or from the bottom of a column, to another column. This move must be made in descending order and in alternating suit colors.

HEARTS

● When you first launch Hearts, you will be asked to join the **Hearts Network** by entering your name.

● When you have done so, select one of the options explained below, then click on the **OK** button. A new game, with four players, will open.

● The aim of the game is to avoid taking tricks containing any hearts or the Queen of Spades. The game ends when a player scores 100 points or over, or when the dealer quits.

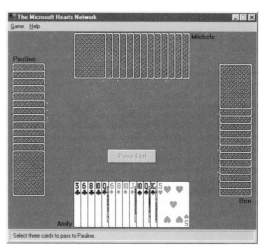

Using the online playing options

If you are connected to the internet, Hearts will give you the option of playing a game online against other players connected to the **Hearts Network**. If you want to join an existing game, select **I want to connect to another game**. If you want to begin a new game, select **I want to be dealer** and wait for others to join. If you would prefer to play against the computer select **I want to be dealer** and press **F2**.

HOW TO PLAY HEARTS

To win, you must have the lowest score at the end of the game. You score points at the end of a hand – one point for each heart, and 13 points for the Queen of Spades. You can "shoot the moon" by winning all the hearts and the queen of spades in a single hand. You score zero points and your opponents are penalized 26 points.

Begin by selecting three cards to pass to the player on your left by clicking on them. Each player passes three cards, and the person with the two of clubs starts by playing it. Play moves clockwise, each player putting down one card of the same suit (or any card if you don't have one). You cannot play a heart or the Queen of Spades in the first round. Once everyone has played a card, the person who put down the highest value card of the leading suit takes the cards (known as a trick). That person then begins play again by leading with a card (you cannot lead with a heart unless a heart was played in the previous round).

MINESWEEPER

● A new game will open when you launch **Minesweeper**, and you can select **New** from the **Game** menu at any time to start a new game.

● To start the timer, and the game, click on any square in the grid.

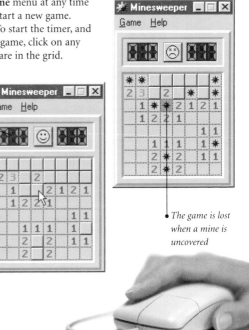

The mine counter

The game is lost when a mine is uncovered

HOW TO PLAY MINESWEEPER

Minesweeper consists of a gridlike playing area that is made up of squares. A number of mines – indicated by the mine counter – are hidden under the squares, and the object of the game is to discover all the mines within the shortest possible time, but without uncovering them. Click on a square to uncover it. Remember, however, that as soon as you uncover a mine, the game is lost. Right-click on a square that you suspect is covering a mine to mark it. When a number appears on a square, it tells you there are that number of mines in the eight squares that surround it. If you are unsure whether a square is covering a mine, then you can right-click on it twice to give it a question mark. When you feel more confident about what the square may contain, right-click it again to mark it as a mine, or right-click it twice to uncover it.

SOLITAIRE

● A new game will open when you launch **Solitaire**, and you can select **Deal** from the **Game** menu at any time to start a new game.

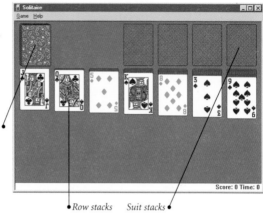

Deck

Row stacks *Suit stacks*

HOW TO PLAY SOLITAIRE

Similar to **Freecell**, **Solitaire** is another single-player card game where the object is to stack the four suits in ascending order. If there is an ace visible on the top of one of the row stacks, click on it to move it to one of the free spaces in the top right of the screen (the suit stacks). Click on any further aces, followed by any cards that can be added to your suit stacks, e.g. a two, then a three, and so on, remembering that cards must be stacked in their suits. When you can make no further moves, click on the deck to turn over a card. This card then comes into play. To make further cards from the row stacks available, you can move cards between row stacks. As opposed to suit stacks, cards in the row stacks are stacked in descending order, and alternate between black cards and red cards.

SOLITAIRE SCORING

If you want to use a scoring system for your Solitaire game, click on the **Game** menu, then choose **Options**, and then choose from **Standard**, or **Vegas**. With **Standard** scoring, you gain or lose points. For a full breakdown of the standard scoring system, select **Help Topics** from the **Help** menu. Under **Contents**, click on **Choosing a scoring system**, and then click on **Standard**. With **Vegas** scoring, you aim to win back money on a 52-dollar bet, earning 5 dollars for every card you play on a suit stack.

COMPUTER GAMING

Of all the multimedia options to be discovered on your computer, games are probably the most exciting, enthralling, and, potentially, the most addictive!

DECIDING WHAT GAMES TO PLAY

No matter what your taste, there will be a game available to interest and excite you – from computerized versions of traditional card games to hi-tech action adventures full of suspense. Listed below is a brief overview of the most popular gaming categories from which to choose – some games even combine several of these genres into one to provide a truly rounded experience.

ARCADE
Exactly as the name suggests, the games in this category include arcade game favorites that have made the transition to the home PC, although most have been completely updated. One of the most popular in this format is the fighting game, involving martial-arts combat with your opponent.

SPORTS
Whatever your favorite sport – football, basketball, tennis, or even fishing – there is likely to be a computerized version available that offers you the chance to participate. Although sports games are particularly suited to competing against a friend, you can also choose to play against your computer.

ROLE-PLAYING ADVENTURE

Much like an action game, you make your way through a world in the guise of a given character, but here you may find yourself in situations influenced far more by your own personal characteristics. For example, the outcome of the game could depend on how you instruct your character to interact with someone they meet.

The World Within
Excitement and tests of skill await you.

SIMULATION

There's no limit to the technology or the make-believe worlds that you can control from your PC. Probably the most popular simulators are those that let you race a powerful car or fly a fighter jet. However, simulations can also include more complicated scenarios, such as playing the mayor of an imaginary city.

STRATEGY

A lot of strategy games revolve around a war scenario, where you have to use tactics and cunning in your command of a battle. Of course, like arcade games, traditional strategy board games have also been updated and turned into immaculate 3D computer versions.

SHOOTING (OR "SHOOT 'EM UP")

This type of game generally involves moving through a location or habitat while shooting at anything that gets in your way. At the same time, something is usually trying to kill *you*. This generally takes place in the "first person," which means that your viewpoint in the game represents exactly what your character is seeing.

ACTION

In this category, you are put in control of a character, who usually has a mission or task to complete. These very absorbing games take you through many exciting and surprising situations – much like an action movie – and often build the tension with a gripping plot and an emotive musical soundtrack.

INSTALLING A CD-ROM GAME

The games mentioned on the previous pages are generally supplied on a CD-ROM, sometimes more than one if it is a particularly complicated game. Although it would initially appear that you simply insert the CD-ROM and play, in actual fact the game requires you to install files on your hard drive first. This is so that complex graphics and certain stages of the game can be loaded more quickly (your computer's hard drive runs much faster than the CD-ROM drive). Because these files can take up a lot of space on your computer – often 100 to 300 Mb for each game – it is essential that you manage the installation of your games effectively. By doing so, you will be able to find and remove games that you are no longer playing to make room for newer acquisitions. The installation process will be clearly explained when you insert your CD-ROM game into your computer, but the steps will look slightly different from game to game. Therefore, the following guidelines focus on the generic instructions that you will have to give your computer no matter which game you are installing.

1 RUNNING THE CD-ROM

● Insert the CD-ROM into your computer and wait for it to run automatically.
● Select to install the game by clicking on the relevant button.

What if the CD-ROM doesn't run…
Double-click on the **My Computer** icon on the desktop, then double-click on the icon for the CD-ROM (usually the **D: drive**). The CD-ROM will either start running or open a folder within which you can double-click on the game icon.

WINDOWS MILLENNIUM EDITION

The update to Windows 98 – Windows ME (Millennium Edition) – is designed specifically for the home computer user and has many facilities devoted to entertainment and gaming.

2 CHOOSING THE LOCATION

● You will be asked where you would like the files to be saved.

● By default, the computer will suggest the **Program Files** folder.

● Click on the **Next** button.

● All the files relating to your game will be contained in one folder.

● You can rename this folder if you wish by typing into the **Program Folders** field, or leave the default name as it is.

● Click on the **Next** button.

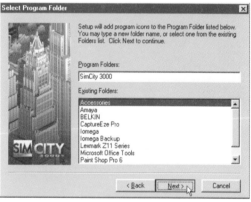

3 INSTALLING THE SOFTWARE

● Once all the settings are confirmed, click on **Next** to proceed with the installation.

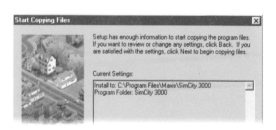

4 EXITING THE INSTALLATION

● Once the installation is complete, click on the **Finish** button.

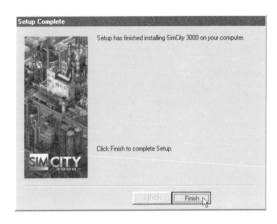

PLAYING A CD-ROM GAME

Once your games are installed on your computer, they can be launched from the **Programs** menu like any other application. However, unlike most other programs, not all the files from the CD-ROM will have been transferred to your computer, so you will need to insert the CD-ROM each time you play the game.

1 LAUNCHING THE GAME

● Click on the **Start** button and select **Programs**, followed by the folder containing your game.

● Click on the game to launch it.

● If you have not already inserted the CD-ROM into your computer, you will be prompted to do so.

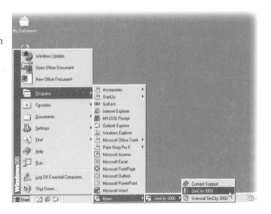

2 STARTING THE GAME

● The game will then start running.

● Many games have some kind of introductory video sequence, but if you prefer to bypass this you can usually do so by clicking anywhere on the screen.

© 1999 Electronic Arts. All Rights Reserved.

3 PLAYING THE GAME

● Of course, all games differ in the way they operate, but you will usually be presented with a screen offering you options to start a new game, load a saved game, or modify the controls and settings.

● Once the game is underway, you will usually be provided with options that allow you to save, pause, or quit the game at any time.

The game shown here – SimCity 3000 – involves building and sustaining your own city.

DOWNLOADING GAMES AND DEMOS

In addition to games that are supplied on CD-ROMs, there is an abundance of games to download to your PC from the internet, along with cheats and hints for just about every computer game created. Gaming is a major subject on the internet, and sites specializing in it are easy to find. Much of the information is posted on the internet by die-hard gaming fans, as well as official sources, and you don't have to go very much farther than one of the major search engines to start finding it. Try the links to games on **Yahoo.com** and in the web directory of **Excite.com,** for example. Most games available for download are demos of newly released games, or games that are currently in production, so this is a great way to try out the latest games before deciding whether to buy them or not. One of the major international sites offering reviews and downloads is **www.gamesdomain.com**.

1 CONNECTING TO THE SITE

● Type **www.gamesdomain. com** into the address panel of your browser and click on the **Go** button.
● The GamesDomain home page will open, displaying links to its latest features.

2 SELECTING DOWNLOADS

● Next, click on the **Downloads** link, and you will be directed to a page listing a wide range of different games.

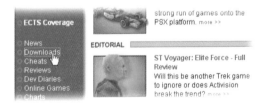

3 SELECTING A GAME

● Select a demo game from the list by clicking on it.

4 SELECTING A LOCATION

● GamesDomain will ask you where you would like to download the file from.
● Click on one of the country names to select it.

● The **File Download** window will appear.
● Make sure that you have selected the radio button next to **Save this file to disk** and click the **OK** button.
● You will now have to choose a location to save the file (a good idea is to create a location on **My Computer** called **Downloads**) after which the download will start.
● A window will appear showing the progress.

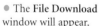

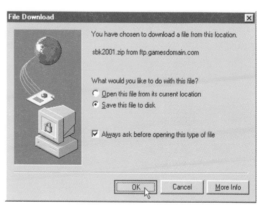

INSTALLING AND PLAYING DOWNLOADS

Just like any other computer game, those that you download will also need installing before you can play them. Downloaded games may be transferred to your computer in a variety of formats but, because they are so large, will commonly be compressed, requiring you to expand the files before you can use them. You should equip your computer with WinZip – a decompression program – before attempting to install your downloaded games (see box below).

1 DECOMPRESSING THE FILES

● Locate the downloaded file on your computer.
● With WinZip installed, your computer will recognize it as a compressed file, and it should display the WinZip "vise" icon.
● Right-click on the icon and select **Extract to folder...** from the pop-up menu.
● A window will appear, showing that the files are being extracted.

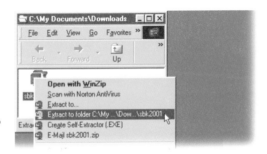

OBTAINING AND INSTALLING WINZIP

A free evaluation version of WinZip is available from www.winzip.com. Select the download option and follow the links until the file is copied to your computer. After the download has completed, double-click on the .exe file. A series of windows will appear as the installation takes place – simply keep clicking on **Next** to continue. When prompted, choose to run with **WinZip Classic**. You can close WinZip after the installation is complete.

2 OPENING THE NEW FOLDER

● When the files have been decompressed, they will be contained in a new folder that can now be found in the same location as your original downloaded file.

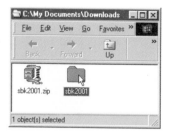

3 LAUNCHING THE SETUP PROGRAM

● Locate the **Setup.exe** file within the new folder and double-click on it to launch it.

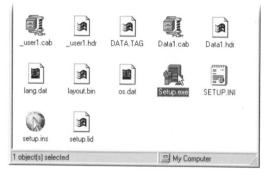

4 STARTING THE SETUP

● A **Welcome** screen appears that will give you some general information. You should read this before proceeding.

● Click on the **Next** button.

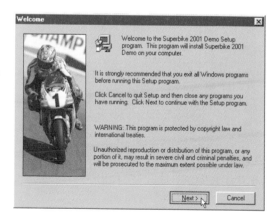

● You will see a series of installation screens similar to those shown on pages 29–30 . Read the information on each one and keep clicking on the **Next** buttons to proceed.
● The game will begin to install.

5 LAUNCHING THE GAME

● Once the installation is complete, click on the **Start** button and locate the folder containing the game in the **Programs** menu.
● Click on the name of the game to launch it.

6 PLAYING THE GAME

● Select any options that you wish to make from the introductory screens, then select **Start** to begin the game.

Superbike 2001 allows you to race a motorbike around some of the world's most famous tracks.

SIGNING UP FOR ONLINE GAMING

Powerful computers and faster modems have meant that playing games over the internet has become increasingly popular. You can choose to play single-player games or, more excitingly, play against other online competitors who are connected to the same site. The Zone is Microsoft's online gaming site (you can find others by performing a web search), and it is worth registering to gain access to all the facilities that the Zone offers (otherwise, you will only be able to play single-player games).

1 BECOMING A MEMBER
● Type **www.zone.com** into the address bar of your browser and click on the **Go** button.
● When the Zone web page is displayed, click on the **New to the Zone?** icon.

● On the next page, click on the **Free Zone Membership** link.

2 STARTING THE SIGN-UP PROCESS
● The **Zone.com signup** page tells you what stages are involved in signing up and, if you prefer, offers the choice of playing games that require no registration.
● Click on the **Start** button to begin the sign-up process.

3 CHOOSING A NAME

● You will be asked to choose a Zone name. With so many players on the Zone, the obvious choices (such as your name) are seldom available. But you can pick a more obscure name or ask the Zone to suggest available names by clicking on **Random Zone Names**.

● Click on a name to select, and it will appear in the **Create Zone Name** field.

● Next, you need to enter a password that will allow you access to the Zone when you sign-in. Type your password in the **Create Password** field and click on **Continue**.

(underscores).
● Your Zone Name must start with a letter or _ (underscore).
● Your Zone Name must be 15 characters or less in length.

If you have trouble finding a name, we can suggest some Random Zone Names for you that are guaranteed to be available.

Here are Some Possibilities

To the right are 5 Zone Names that are currently available. If you don't like any of them, we'll be happy to find five other Zone Names for you.

Or you can enter a Zone Name of your own.

Here are some Zone Names you might like to use:

Arrested_Drake
Appointed_Pilot
BalancedPrawn
Ample_Mercury
Awestruck_Hook

Create Zone Name
Appointed_Pilot
Create Password
·············

Continue

4 ENTERING YOUR CONTACT DETAILS

● On the next page, enter an email address in the **E-mail** field that the Zone can use to contact you.

● Click on the **Continue** button.

By entering your e-mail address in the box below you are indicating you are 13 years of age or older. If you are under 13, please leave this box blank.

E-mail
·········@·········.co.uk

Continue

☐ Yes, please send me the Zone newsletter and special event and tournament announcements

5 DOWNLOADING CORE ZONE FILES

● Files that you require to use the Zone now need to be downloaded to your computer.

● Click on the **Start Download** button.

The downloads will take approximately 5 minutes using a 28.8k modem.

After you click the start download button, you may see a dialog box. Depending on your browser's security settings, this dialog box may ask you to confirm the download. This is normal.

Start Download

● You may see a security warning appear during the download process. This is normal, and you can simply confirm that you want the download to proceed.

● When you see a Spade icon appear on screen, the download has been completed.

● Click on the **Click here when you see the Spade** button.

Download In Progress

This download should take approximately 5 minutes on a 28.8k modem. You will see various progress dialogs displayed on the screen during the installation. When the download is complete, you will see a picture of a Spade below.

If after 5 minutes you do not see a picture of the Spade, visit our help page.

Click here when you see the Spade

The first time you visit a game on the Zone, additional game components may need to be installed. This will happen automatically, and only the first time you visit the game room.

6 VIEWING THE TUTORIAL

● Once your sign-up with the Zone is confirmed, you are ready to enter the Zone.

● It is a good idea at this stage to work your way through the short tutorial so that you become familiar with how the Zone works.

● Click on the **Show me the tutorial, then take me to the games** link.

● The tutorial will open, and you can view any of the 15 pages by clicking on the links or the buttons at the bottom of the screen.

● When you have finished, close the tutorial and log on.

You have successfully created a new Zone Name

Zone Name: Appointed_Pilot
Password: Over_And_Out

After you click the top link below, a Zone logon dialog box will appear. In this box, you must type your Zone Name and password. This box is the only dialog you will see when you return to the Zone in the future.

If you are new to the Zone, we recommend that you follow our tutorial. It will teach you all you need to know to play on the Zone. Going through the tutorial will take approximately five minutes.

Logon and take me to the games

Show me the tutorial, then take me to the games

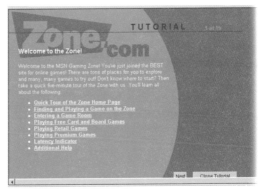

7 INSTALLING ZONE SOFTWARE

● When you log on for the first time, your computer will automatically install the Gaming Zone software.

● When prompted, click on the **Install** button and follow any other instructions that appear on screen. You will be asked to accept a license agreement during this process.

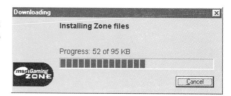

8 LOGGING ON TO THE ZONE

● Once the installation is complete, the **Sign In** window will appear.

● Enter your **Password** and click on the **OK** button.

● When you see the welcome screen, click on the **Home** link to go to the main Zone page.

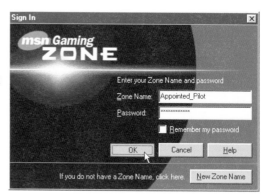

Launching the Zone in the future
Once installed, you can launch the Zone directly by clicking on the **Start** button and selecting **MSN Gaming Zone** from the **Programs** menu.

PLAYING GAMES ONLINE

There is a wide range of games to choose from in the Zone – primarily traditional card and strategy games. However, you can also challenge players online using some retail games by inserting your CD-ROM game into your computer and then linking up with someone who is playing the same game.

1 SELECTING A GAME TO PLAY

● On the Zone's home page you will see a list of links to "gaming rooms" – currently occupied by the number of online players indicated (this is a good way of finding out which games are currently most popular).

● Decide which game you would like to play and click on a link. **Chess** has been chosen in this instance.

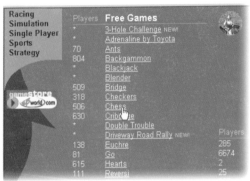

2 CHOOSING A GAMING ROOM

● Each game has a variety of "rooms" for you to join, and these are divided into categories based on experience.

● As a newcomer to the Zone, select one of the rooms that is suitable for casual or beginner gameplay.

● Once you have selected a room, your computer will automatically install any files that are required for the game you are playing.

3 ENTERING THE GAMING ROOM

● The gaming room will open, as may the **Zone Tips** dialog box. Read the tips, then click on **OK**.

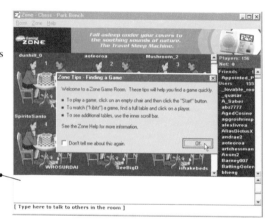

The panel at the bottom of the screen allows you to have a conversation with other players in the room

4 VIEWING A GAME IN PROGRESS

● The room is made up of a series of tables.

● Tables with two players present indicate that a game is in progress, and you can simply look in on (or *kibitz*) the game by clicking on one of the players.

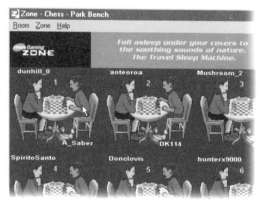

● A box will appear asking you to confirm that you want to watch the game.
● Click on the **Yes** button.

● The game in play will open, and you will be able to see each move the players make.

The eyes icon indicates that the game is being watched by a spectator – in this case, you

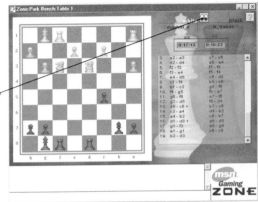

5 PARTICIPATING IN A GAME

● To take part in a game yourself, find a table with one player resident and click on the empty chair to join them.
● Click on the **Start** button to begin the game.
● Alternatively, you can click on a chair at an empty table and wait for someone to join you.

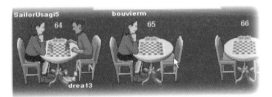

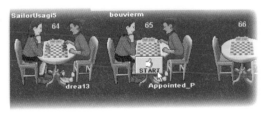

CD-ROM AND DVD

Games aside, CD-ROMs and DVDs can provide some of the most interactive and exciting experiences on your PC, be it learning a new language or watching a blockbuster movie.

DIFFERENT TYPES OF CD-ROM

CD-ROMs are disks crammed with huge amounts of information that take advantage of all that multimedia has to offer. Depending on the subject, a CD-ROM is likely to include a full mix of video footage, animation, games, and music. You will also often find links that launch your web browser automatically and take you to related internet sites.

WHAT'S AVAILABLE?

There is a CD-ROM available on almost any subject, and one of the main advantages of their interactive format is that they make education fun. Take, for example, the 20th century. A conventional book on this subject would simply offer text and pictures, but a CD-ROM can add video and news broadcasts, interviews, voice-overs, and interactive quizzes. Of course, not all CD-ROMs are strictly educational. Some help you to landscape your garden or redesign the interior of your house. Others are part of a conventional music CD, so you can watch videos of some of the tracks, or other exclusive footage of the artist. They are very commonly used as promotional items so expect to find disks attached to the covers of magazines, and even sent through the post as direct mail.

What does CD-ROM stand for?

CD-ROM means *Compact Disk Read-Only Memory*. In other words, the disk contains information that can be read but not overwritten (unlike a floppy disk, for example).

USING A CD-ROM

Just like a game CD-ROM , other kinds of interactive CD-ROM that you run will first require some files to be installed on to your computer as part of a setup procedure. These enable the contents of the CD-ROM to be accessed more quickly, but the files, which can be very large, can take up a considerable amount of room on your hard disk. It is therefore wise to remove files that you no longer use.

1 SETTING UP THE CD-ROM
● Insert the CD-ROM into your computer and wait for it to start running.
● When the welcome screen appears, click on the **Next** button to proceed.
● You will see a series of installation screens similar to those shown on pages 29–30 . Keep clicking on the **Next** buttons.
● The CD-ROM setup program will run.

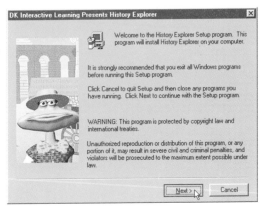

2 RUNNING THE CD-ROM
● Once the installation is complete, click on the **Start** button and locate the folder containing the CD-ROM files in the **Programs** menu.
● Highlight the title of the CD-ROM to launch it.

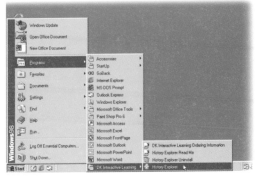

3 GETTING STARTED

● Most CD-ROMs are very well designed and begin by introducing the contents of the disk, and explaining what you need to do.

This example is an educational CD-ROM for children, called **History Explorer**.

4 USING THE CD-ROM

● To progress through the disk, nearly all CD-ROMs simply require you to make choices using one click of the mouse, or by entering details with the keyboard.

PLAYING A DVD MOVIE

A Digital Video Disc (DVD) looks like a CD-ROM but has a much larger storage capacity – enough to store a feature-length movie. DVD videos have better picture and sound quality than a video tape, and can also offer extra features – for example, you can select different camera angles or view behind-the-scenes footage.

1 INSTALLING SOFTWARE

● Insert the movie disk into the DVD-ROM drive on your computer.
● A window may appear, asking whether you would like to install the PC features. Click on **Install**.
● On the following screen click the **Next** button to proceed (you may also be offered a chance to install a player during this process).

DVD player software
If you find that you require a DVD player, you can download **WinDVD** from www. intervideoinc.com.

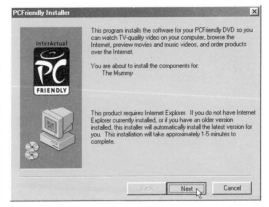

COMPUTER COMPATIBILITY

You may only have a standard CD-ROM drive fitted – check the system spec of your computer to find out whether you have a DVD-ROM drive. If you are buying a new PC, then consider buying one with a DVD-ROM drive. DVD games will surely become more common and, with the increased capacity that DVD offers, promise to include some exciting new features.

2 SELECTING THE MENU OPTIONS

● The disk will start to run, and a menu screen will appear. In the example we are viewing Universal Pictures' *The Mummy*.
● In addition to the movie itself there will be other options, such as games and information on the cast.
● Click on one of the options, in this case – **Behind the Scenes**.

● Information and/or video footage will appear on screen. There may also be further links to related topics.

● When you have explored your selected area of information, you can return to the main menu.
● There will be a link somewhere on the page, such as **Back to the Home Page**. Click on the link.

3 PLAYING THE MOVIE

● When you want to watch the film itself, click on **Play Movie** in the main menu screen.

● The movie will start playing.
● There will also be a control panel accessible, offering basic functions such as **Stop**, **Pause**, **Rewind**, and **Fast Forward**. Often, more advanced functions will be available, allowing you to skip to key scenes in the film and display subtitles.

WATCHING MOVIE TRAILERS ON THE INTERNET

You can keep track of the latest movie releases without a DVD-ROM drive. As the internet is such a good marketing device, most movie companies launch a website devoted to a new release. These sites are easy to find – simply type the movie name into a search engine. They nearly always include some video footage, usually the movie trailer. When you click on the movie preview link, the video will take a few minutes to download to your computer, and you can then view the footage using Windows Media Player.

COMMUNICATE IN STYLE

The internet and email provide endless possibilities for exchanging beautifully designed interactive messages and greetings with your friends and family.

SENDING A VIRTUAL POSTCARD

By combining the internet and email there is now no need to send boring, text-only, messages to your friends and family. There are many sites available that give you the opportunity to send exciting, colorful, greetings, known as "virtual postcards," via the web. Try the home page of your Internet Service Provider for a start. In this example, we are using a site called **www.postcards.org**, which provides a vast array of pictures to which you can add your own messages. You can even choose an animated card, and add music to your greeting. Once you have sent your card, the recipient will receive an email message informing them that there is a card waiting for them. They will be provided with a web address that will direct them to your card, and they will see it in their browser exactly as you composed it.

1 CONNECTING TO THE SITE

● Type **www. postcards.org** in the address panel of your internet browser and click on **Go**.

● The 1001 Postcards site will load and appear on screen.

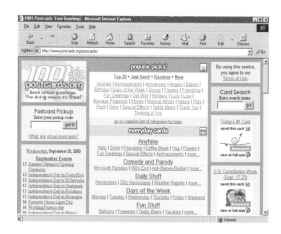

2 CHOOSING A CATEGORY

● Decide which type of card you want to send. There are many available, ranging from birthday greetings to cards that are humorous or simply contain beautiful pictures. Some are even animated.

● Click on a category.

3 SELECTING A CARD

● The page will display a selection of cards for you to choose from.

● When you have decided which card you would like to send, click on its preview.

1001 Postcards Home » Topics » Celebrations »

Anniversary

Postcards by page: [prev | 1 | 2 | next]

send this card ✉   send this card ✉   send this card ✉

Animated!   Animated!   Animated!

view at full-size 📷   view at full-size 📷   view at full-size 📷

4 VIEWING THE CARD

● Your chosen card will be displayed at a larger size. If you want to change your selected card, click on the **Back** button in your browser and choose again.

● When you have selected a card, click on the **send this postcard** button.

Happy Anniversary*

postcard courtesy of Jeff Victor

send this postcard!   find similar cards

* you can change the title of this card when you send it

5 COMPOSING YOUR CARD

● A page will open displaying a series of boxes into which you enter the destination details.

● Begin by entering the recipient's email address, and, in the second box, their name.

● Then enter your email address and name.

● Scroll down the page to view the other fields.

1001 Postcards Home »
Personalize Your Postcard!

To personalize your postcard, answer the questions below!

Animated!

What is *their email address*?
Enter up to 9 addresses, separated by commas.
(e.g. clark@kent.com, lois@lane.edu)
name@recipient's_destination.com

What is *their name*?
(e.g. Aunt Edna)
Sarah & Michael

What is *your email address*?
(e.g. your_name@whatever.net)
name@sender's_destination.com

What is *your name*?
(e.g. Cool Dude)
Andy

● Next, enter a title for the card, or you can leave the default title as it is.

● Then, type a message (you can check your spelling, if you wish, by clicking the **spell check** button).

● You can personalize the card further by selecting a piece of music to accompany your card, and a theme, which adds a background image behind the card itself.

What is the *title* of your card?
(It's optional, and appears above the card.)
Happy Anniversary

What is *your message*?
(this one's up to you!)
Best wishes on your anniversary

spell check

What *music* would you like to send?
(pick a song, or choose 'no music')
Happy Together

listen to this song

What *theme* do you want to use?
(changes the way the whole page looks)
Abstract   demo theme

6 PREVIEWING THE CARD

● Decide when you would like the card to be sent – you can provide a date or choose to send the card immediately.

● Click in the check boxes if you want to take advantage of any of the other options.

● Once you have entered all the details, click on the **preview before sending** button.

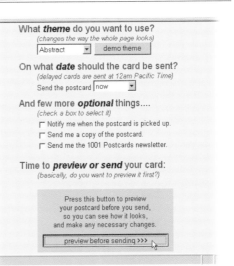

7 SENDING YOUR CARD

● Your completed greeting will appear, including your messages. You should also be able to hear the music that you assigned to the card.

● If you want to change anything, click on the **make changes** button.

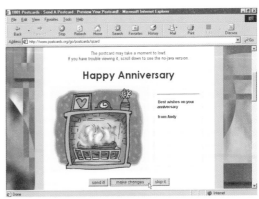

● Once you are happy with your greeting, click on the **send it!** button.

YOUR CREATIVE PC

**Having fun on your computer needn't be an unproductive
activity. In addition to education and entertainment,
you can use your PC to develop your creative talents.**

DRAWING AND PAINTING

While there are many drawing and
painting software packages available to
purchase – many of which are highly
advanced – Windows 98 provides you
with the means to create quite impressive
pieces of artwork, and even gives you the
option of applying your creations to your
desktop screen as a "wallpaper."

1 LAUNCHING WINDOWS PAINT
● Click on the **Start** button
and then select **Programs**,
followed by **Accessories**,
then **Paint**.

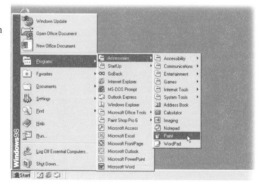

2 ENLARGING THE WINDOW
● When **Paint** opens,
you may want to enlarge
the window so that you
can see the full area of
your "canvas."
● Click in the bottom right
corner of the window and
hold down the mouse
button while you drag the
window to a larger size.

3 BEGINNING YOUR PICTURE

● To get accustomed to drawing with the mouse, experiment by sketching with the **Pencil**.

● You can undo an action at any time by selecting **Undo** from the **Edit** menu, or by holding down the Ctrl and **Z** keys.

● When you feel confident, draw a rough outline of your picture.

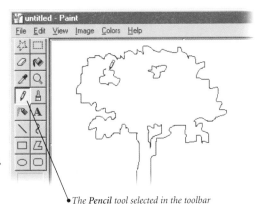

●*The Pencil tool selected in the toolbar*

4 USING THE OTHER TOOLS

● Just as you would progress your drawing conventionally when using paper and paint, begin to work on your picture using the other tools, such as the **Brush** and the **Airbrush**.

The Airbrush tool ●

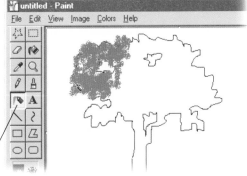

SELECTING DIFFERENT COLORS

You can choose to work with a different color at any time by making a selection from the palette at the bottom of the **Paint** window. Click on a color swatch to activate it.

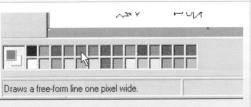

Draws a free-form line one pixel wide.

● Notice that when you select a tool, you can also alter its size by clicking in the options provided underneath the toolbar.

● To work in more detail, use the **Magnifier** to zoom in on parts of your picture.

5 CORRECTING MISTAKES

● The beauty of drawing and painting on a computer is the facility to correct mistakes as many times as you like.

● Select the **Eraser**, adjust its size to your needs, and click and drag it over the areas of your picture that you want to remove.

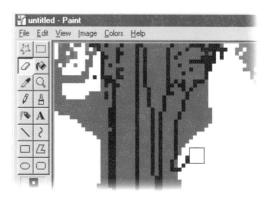

6 COMPLETING YOUR PICTURE

● Once you have completed your picture, select **Save As** from the **File** menu and save it to a location on your computer.

SETTING YOUR PICTURE AS WALLPAPER

Once you have completed your work of art, Paint gives you the option of applying your picture to the desktop screen as a "wallpaper." This provides you with the perfect opportunity to use your PC as a gallery, allowing you to show off your most recent creations to friends and family whenever they use the computer.

APPLYING THE WALLPAPER

● With your finished picture open in Paint, click on the **File** menu and select **Set As Wallpaper** (**Tiled**) to create a repeat pattern of your picture across the screen, or **Set As Wallpaper** (**Centered**) to fill the screen.

● Your picture will instantly appear on the desktop screen and you can close the Paint program.

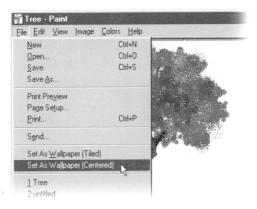

REMOVING YOUR WALLPAPER PICTURE

When you no longer want to have your picture on display on the desktop, you can replace it with one of the standard Windows 98 screens. Right-click on the desktop and select **Properties** from the pop-up menu. Click on the **Background** tab, then scroll to the top of the Wallpaper list and highlight (**None**). Click on **OK** to revert back to the standard green background. Alternatively, you can choose any one of the other options in the list.

DESIGNING YOUR OWN ICONS

In addition to creating your own desktop screens , you can personalize your computer even further by creating your own icons, and then applying them to folders on your computer. You can do this using Microangelo – a program that lets you draw icons in a specific format. It is easy to obtain over the internet .

1 LAUNCHING STUDIO

● Click on the **Start** button and select **Programs**, followed by **Microangelo**, then **Studio**.
● The **Microangelo Studio** window will open.

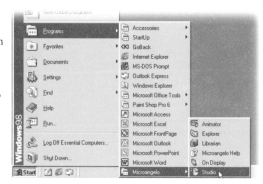

2 CREATING YOUR ICON

● Using the same techniques as drawing a picture in Paint , begin to create your icon. You will notice that there are similar tools available as in Paint – a pencil, brush, etc.
● The only restriction this time is that you are confined to a pixel "grid." It is a good idea to use the grid to plan the design of your icon and fill in the squares of the grid accordingly.

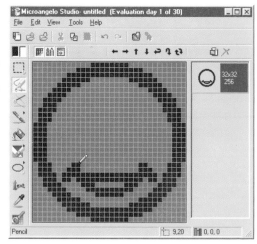

3 SELECTING A COLOR

● To choose another color, click on **View** and select **Color Palette** from the drop-down menu. The palette will open, and you simply click on a color swatch to select it.

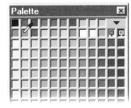

● You can fill whole areas with color by using the **Flood tool**.

Obtaining Microangelo…
Microangelo is available on the internet to buy, or as a 30-day evaluation version. Connect to **http://download.cnet.com** and enter **Microangelo** into the **Search** box. From here, you will be directed to a page where you will be able to download the software.

● *Fill whole areas with the color of your choice*

4 COMPLETING YOUR ICON

● Add detail to your icon by drawing in some highlights or shadows. It is surprising how much detail will appear in an icon, even at such a small size (take a look at the existing icons on your computer for inspiration).

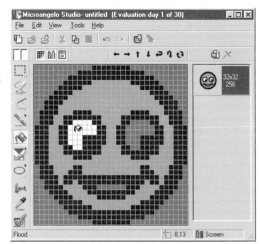

5 SAVING YOUR ICON

● Once you have completed your icon, select **Save As** from the **File** menu.
● The **Save As** window will appear.

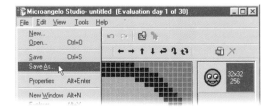

● Select a location in which to save the file and give your new icon a name.
● In the **Save as type** panel, ensure that **Icon Resource** is selected.
● Click on the **Save** button, and then close Microangelo Studio.

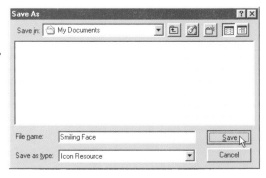

APPLYING YOUR NEW ICONS

Once you have created your icons, you will need to use another part of Microangelo in order to apply them to the folders of your choice. Microangelo On Display manages the application of icons to folders and directories. It can also help you get everything back to normal if you go a bit too wild and need to retreat!

1 LAUNCHING ENGINEER

● Click on the **Start** button and select **Programs**, followed by **Microangelo**, then **On Display**.
● The **Microangelo On Display** window will open.

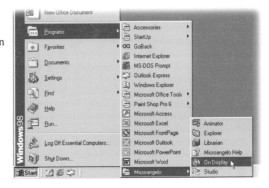

2 SELECTING A FOLDER

● In this example we are going to apply our new icon to the **Documents** folder, so click on the **Start Menu** tab and then select **Documents** from the list by highlighting it.
● Click on the **Change** button.

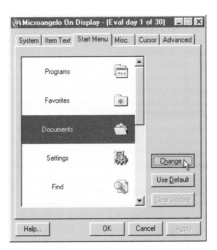

3 CHANGING THE ICON

● In the **Open** window, locate your new icon file and click on it to select it.
● Click on the **Open** button.

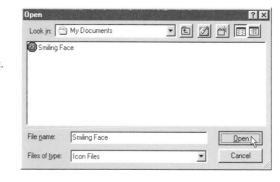

● Your new icon will now be displayed in the **Change Icon** window.
● Select the icon and click on the **OK** button.

4 APPLYING THE ICON

● You will now be returned to the **Microangelo On Display** window, where you will see your new icon assigned to the **Documents** folder.
● Click on the **OK** button.

A green cross appears to indicate that the new icon has been assigned

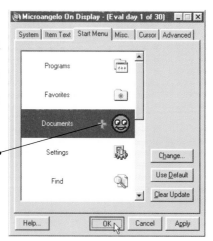

● When you return to the
desktop you will be able to
view the result of the icon
change.

● In this case the new icon
is displayed next to the
Documents folder in the
Start menu.

5 REVERTING TO NORMAL

● At some point, you may
want to remove your icon
from a folder, and revert to
the default Windows 98
icon.

● To do this, open
Microangelo On Display
and highlight the folder in
the list.

● This time click on the
Use Default button.

● Microangelo will
automatically reassign the
default icon to the folder.

● Click on **OK**.

RECORDING SOUNDS

You will have already noticed that your computer gives off a variety of sounds to indicate when certain things are happening, or to inform you that you have made an error. All of these sounds can be changed, and Windows 98 gives you plenty of standard sounds from which to choose. However, more fun can be had from recording your own sounds, and applying them to specific actions. For example, why not make your own recording that plays whenever someone makes a mistake? For added effect, apply the sound to the computer when no one else is around, ready to surprise them the next time they use the PC!

1 CONNECTING A MICROPHONE
● Plug a compatible microphone into the relevant port on your computer.

2 LAUNCHING SOUND RECORDER
● Click on the **Start** button and select **Programs** from the drop-down menu, followed by **Accessories**, then **Entertainment**.
● Within the **Entertainment** menu, select **Sound Recorder**.
● The **Sound Recorder** window will open.

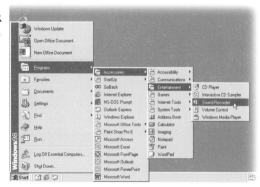

3 BEGINNING THE RECORDING

● Click on the **Record** button and begin to make your recording. Keep the recording short, since a long alert sound will become very annoying.

● *The Record button*

4 COMPLETING THE RECORDING

● As soon as you have finished, click on the **Stop** button. Try to avoid any long delays between finishing the recording and stopping, since any blank spaces will also be recorded.

● Press the **Play** button to make sure that you are happy with the result.

● If you would like to make your recording again to obtain a better result, for example, select **New** from the **File** menu.

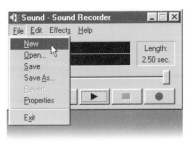

● When you are asked whether you would like to save changes, click on the **No** button.

● Repeat steps 3 and 4.

5 SAVING YOUR RECORDING

● Click on **File** and select **Save As** from the drop-down menu.

● Choose a location to save the file – a logical place is with the other Windows sound effects. These are found in the **Media** folder within the **Windows** folder of your computer's **C:** drive.

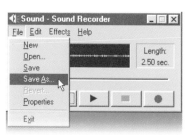

● Give your recording a name and click on **Save**, ensuring that you have selected the **Sounds** (*.wav) format in the **Save as type:** box.

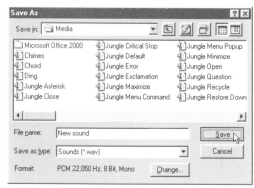

DOWNLOADING SOUNDS FROM THE INTERNET

There are plenty of sound effects to be sourced from the internet by performing a simple search. For example, you could try and find some of your favorite TV character's catch phrases. Once you have downloaded the sound effect, you can apply it to actions and events the same as you would with your own recordings . When looking for sounds, always choose files that end in **.wav** since this is the format that Windows recognizes.

APPLYING SOUNDS TO EVENTS

Once you have saved your recordings on your computer, you will then be able to apply them to actions that you make – known as "events." Your recordings will be able to replace the "chord" or "ding" that Windows 98 offers as standard.

1 OPENING SOUNDS PROPERTIES

● Click on the **Start** button and select **Settings**, followed by **Control Panel** from the menu.
● The **Control Panel** window will open.

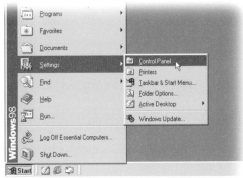

● Double-click on the **Sounds** icon to open the **Sounds Properties** window.

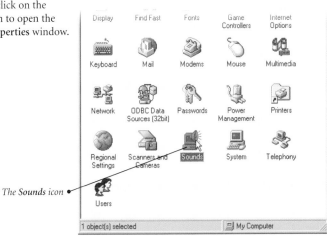

The Sounds icon ●

2 SELECTING THE EVENT

● In the **Events** list, highlight the action to which you want to apply your sound, e.g. **Asterisk** (the general alert sound).

● Click on the **Browse** button to open the **Browse for Asterisk sound** window.

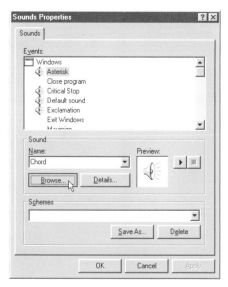

3 CHOOSING YOUR SOUND

● Locate your recording in the **Media** folder ⌐, or wherever your sound is saved, and click on it to select it.

● Click on the **OK** button.

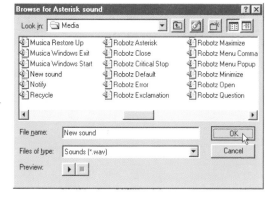

66 Saving your recording

4 PREVIEWING YOUR SOUND

● Your sound will now appear in the **Name** box.
● Click on the **Play** button if you want to preview the sound that you have selected.

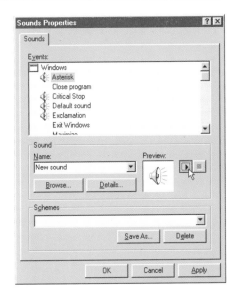

5 APPLYING YOUR SOUND

● Click on the **Apply** button, then press **OK**.
● Now, when you close the **Sounds Properties** box your new sound will play whenever the event is activated.

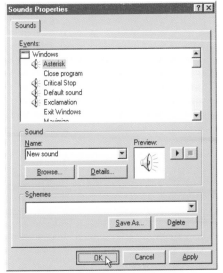

GLOSSARY

BROWSER
A software interface that enables you to view web pages on the internet.

CD-ROM
Compact Disk Read-Only Memory. A disk containing data, such as games and programs. Data can only be read from the disk, not written to it.

CONTROLLER
Any device that plugs into your computer and that is used to perform actions during game playing.

DEMO
A free demonstration version of a game that usually contains one stage from the final version, so that the player can get an idea of what the game is like.

DOWNLOAD
A file that is copied to your computer over the internet from a remote server.

DVD
Digital Versatile (or Video) Disk. A disk with the size and appearance of a compact disk, but with enough storage capacity to contain a high-quality, feature-length movie.

EVENT
An action that takes place on your computer, such as starting up, opening a file, or receiving an email.

GAMEPAD
A handheld device that allows you to control games by using your fingers and thumbs.

GAMES CONSOLE
A machine that plugs into your television set and allows you to play complex games, which have very high-quality graphics.

GAMES ROOM
A location within a gaming website that offers games for you to play against other online competitors.

ICON
A graphic image that is assigned to a computer file so that you can identify the type of file.

INSTALLING
Copying files to locations on your computer, which enable a program or game to run.

JOYSTICK
A one-handed device that offers sensitive control of a variety of games. Particularly suited to flying simulations.

MODEM
MOdulator-DEModulator. A device that connects your computer to the internet. It plugs into the telephone line.

MULTIMEDIA
The term given to the wide range of interactive media available on your computer, including games, CD-ROMs, video, animation, and music.

NETWORK
A number of computers that are connected to each other.

ONLINE GAMING
Playing games over the internet against other online computer users connected to the same site.

PERIPHERALS
Hardware devices that connect to your computer, such as a joystick.

STREAMING
The transfer of video footage over the internet to your computer, which can be viewed immediately, often live.

SOUND RECORDER
An application within Windows 98 that lets you record your own short sounds and save them on your computer.

VIRTUAL POSTCARD
A greeting – consisting of an image, a message, and even music – that is sent via a website to another online computer user.

WALLPAPER
A pattern or picture that can be applied to the desktop of your computer.

WINDOWS MEDIA PLAYER
An application within Windows 98 that allows you to play video footage and listen to audio files.

WINZIP
A program used to extract files from a single compressed "archive," which has been created to save disk space.

ZONE
Microsoft's gaming website, which offers a number of online games, either to be played individually or against other internet users.

INDEX

ACKNOWLEDGMENTS

PUBLISHER'S ACKNOWLEDGMENTS
Dorling Kindersley would like to thank the following:
Activision, Inc., Bungie.com, CNET Networks, Inc., CounterTop Software, Creative
Technology, Ltd., Electronic Arts, Fox Sports®, theglobe.com, inc., Impact Software,
Interplay Entertainment Corp., Postcards.org, Sega.com, Inc., Sony Computer
Entertainment of America, Talonsoft, Universal Pictures

Every effort has been made to trace the copyright holders.
The publisher apologizes for any unintentional omissions and would be pleased,
in such cases, to place an acknowledgment in future editions of this book.

Activision® is a registered trademark of Activision, Inc. © 1998 Activision, Inc.
Asteroids is a trademark of Atari Interactive, Inc. All rights reserved.
SimCity 3000™ © 2000 Electronic Arts Inc. SimCity 3000 and Maxis are trademarks or
registered trademarks of Electronic Arts Inc. in the U.S. and/or other countries. All
rights reserved. Maxis™ is an Electronics Arts™ brand.
"Superbike 2001" (the "Game") is licensed officially by SBK Superbike International
Limited. The Game is not sponsored, endorsed or licensed by any other entities
contained within the Game. All manufacturers, motorcycles, circuits, names, brands
and associated imagery featured in the Game are trademarks of their respective
owners. All rights reserved. Exclusively licensed to and published by Electronic Arts.
"SBK Superbike World Championship" and all its variations, copyrights, trademarks
and images used or associated with the Game are all copyrights and/or trademarks of
SBK Superbike International Limited and are being used under exclusive license by
Electronic Arts Inc. SBK Superbike International Limited is the exclusive promoter of
the FIM Superbike World Championship.